NOV 1 0 2005

EAST MEADOW PUBLIC LIBRARY

D1491244

East Meadow Public Library
1886 Front Street
East Meadow, New York 11554
516-794-2570

BAKER & TAYLOR

Brooklyn Is

FORDHAM UNIVERSITY PRESS NEW YORK 2005

JAMES AGEE

Preface by Jonathan Lethem

Brooklyn Is

Southeast of the Island: Travel Notes

"Southeast of the Island: Travel Notes"
Copyright © 1968 The James Agee Trust

"Agee's Brooklyn"
Copyright © 2005 Jonathan Lethem

All rights reserved. No part of this publication
may be reproduced, stored in a retrieval
system, or transmitted in any form or by any
means—electronic, mechanical, photocopy,
recording, or any other—except for brief
quotations in printed reviews, without the
prior permission of the publisher.

Library of Congress Cataloging-in-Publication Data
is available from the Library of Congress

ISBN 0-8232-2492-9

Printed in the United States of America
07 06 05   5 4 3 2 1
First edition
Designed by Linda Secondari

CONTENTS

AGEE'S BROOKLYN

by Jonathan Lethem

I WANT to try and sing back at James Agee's astonishing song of Brooklyn, this astonishing secret text which like the heart of the borough itself throbs in raw shambolic splendor, never completely discovered, impossible to mistake. Agee is such a loving, explosive, and mournful singer; his prose aims the methods of Walt Whitman like a loving bullet toward the next century, brings that greatest singer of American identity smash up against the midcentury's grubby, boundless polyglot accumulation of successive immigrant hordes, and predicts the outerborough songs to come, the ones that could only have been written by immigrant sons and daughters themselves—Malamud, Fuchs, Paley, Gornick, Marshall—though Agee, much like Whitman, can seem to encompass and predict any author who ever tried to touch Brooklyn since: Henry Miller, Paula Fox, myself. Agee's breath and voice come cresting at us out of the past yet keenly modern, and engaged in every syllable with the tides of the past that rush under the craft of his words—Agee can seem to be surfing the past, always in danger of being swallowed by the high punishing curl of time, always somehow riding atop it instead. Yet if he's a singer he's also a painter, brushstroking with his language the sun-bleached brownstone facades of Slope and Heights and Hill, the shingles and stucco of Flatbush and Greenpoint, the graffiti and commercial signage left like clues for future archeologists—the brush of his prose is as fond and melancholy as Mark Rothko's in his subway paintings or Philip Guston's in his street scenes, before both painters sank their feeling for the city in abstraction. He writes as though drunk on matters of space and geometry and distance, always seeing the life of the city whole and in microscopic miniature at once, and persistently smashing together architecture and emotion, conveying in the grain of a "scornful cornice" or a "blasted mansion" or a "half-made park with the odd pubescent nudity of all new public efforts" or "drawn breathing shades" or an "asphaltic shingle" (his neologism suggesting "asthmatic," "exalted," "sephardic," and who knows what else) his sense that the archipelago of islands settled by the mad invaders of this continent and the refugees who followed, and the nature of the buildings and the streets and the signs the arrivistes constructed everywhere upon these New York islands, are in every way implicated in the experience of any given life lived even temporarily within their bounds, including his own. The shape of the land, in other words—and of the houses and trees and roadways, and the subways now running underneath them—has, in Agee's view, subdued and civilized and corrupted those who had arrived to subdue and civilize and corrupt this place; they made it strange and were made strange by it in turn. Agee tackles head-on Brooklyn's doubleness, the paradox of the borough's weird preening inferiority complex at its proximity to Manhattan and its simultaneous bovine oblivious hugeness, its indifference to attempts at definition—including Agee's own. He nevertheless made himself so open, such a portal for collective presence, that he truly can seem to have managed to allude to every icon of the place, every glorious shred of ruined culture a Brooklynite might ever flatter himself thinking only he'd cherished, and to have mentioned every talismanic name, Ex-Lax, Adelphi, Dekalb, finding vital concrete poetry in the enigma of the names, stitching time together, speaking to every Brooklyn dweller, past or future. In my own instance, Agee paints at one point a devastating cameo of Brooklyn Heights gentility and insularity (subtitled: *the dusk of the Gods*); reporting his snobbish host's fear, that "Negroes" and "Syrians" are "within two blocks of us"; those same "Syrians" now own great swaths of the neighborhood in question, which truly belongs more to them than to any other constituency (and where is the great novel of Arab-American immigrant life on Atlantic Avenue?); they are, in fact, the landlords of the apartment on Bergen Street in which I sit writing this today—so it may seem that Agee is at my shoulder. The essay's prose is, at last, more than tidal, it's cyclonic, as the narrative rises up on the swirling imaged-junked cone of Agee's prophetic style to see the borough and its people whole, diving through parlor windows or into movie theater seats or along a quiet Sunday street to sweep up another handful of lives in a few sprung, compacted sentences, and sweep on. To end at the zoo, a perfect symbol of Agee's ultimate insinuation: that all this mad paving and dressing up and scribbling on walls (or on pages) and pouring tea from china cups is still finally nothing more than a vision of the natural world— that all our cultural outcroppings, chaotic and placid alike, are just evidence of our peculiar animal activities, and that Brooklyn is only a particularly dense and dreamy version of the zoo that is all human life, an enclosure where any number of not terribly imaginative or visionary individuals can collectively realize a great visionary mass result, a kind of vast art installation made by instinctive, consolation-seeking animals, merely by living their beautiful, ordinary, mad lives in adjacency to one another.

Brooklyn, New York
June 2005

Brooklyn Is

Southeast of the Island: Travel Notes

"City of homes and churches."

Whitman, writing of Brooklyn.

"One of the great waste places of the world."

Doughty, writing of Arabia.

"And blights with plagues the marriage hearse."

Blake, writing of London.

"Life is fundamentally composed of vegetable matter."

Obsolete textbook of biology.

WATCHING THEM in the trolleys, or along the in-exhaustible reduplications of the streets of their small tradings and their sleep, one comes to notice, even in the most urgently poor, a curious quality in the eyes and at the corners of the mouths, rela-tive to what is seen on Manhattan Island: a kind of drugged softness or narcotic relaxation. The same look may be seen in monasteries and in the lawns of sanitariums, and there must have been some similar look among soldiers convalescent of shell shock in institutionalized British gardens where, in a late summer dusk, a young man could mistake heat lightnings and the crumpling of hidden thunder for what he has left in France, and must return to. If there were not Manhattan, there could not be this Brooklyn look; for truly to appreciate what one escapes, it must be not only distant but near at hand. Only: all escapes are relative, and bestow their own peculiar forms of bondage.

It is the same of the physique and whole tone and metre of the city itself. You have only to cross a bridge to know it: how behind you the whole of living is drawn up straining into verticals, tightened and badgered in nearly every face of man and child and building; and how where you are entering, even among the riverside throes of mechanisms and of tenements in the iron streets, this whole of living is nevertheless relaxed upon horizontalities, a deep taproot of stasis in each action and each building. Partly, it suggests the qualities of any small American city, the absorption in home, the casualness of the measuredly undistinguished: only this usual provincialism is powerfully enhanced here by the near existence of Manhattan, which has drawn Brooklyn of most of what a city's vital organs are, and upon which an inestimable swarm of Brooklyn's population depends for living itself. And again, this small-city quality is confused in the deep underground atomic drone of the intertextured procedures upon blind time of more hundreds on hundreds of thousands of compacted individual human existences than the human imagination can comprehend or bear to comprehend.

It differs from most cities in this: that though it has perhaps a "center," and hands, and eyes, and feet, it is chiefly no whole or recognizable animal but an exorbitant pulsing mass of scarcely discriminable cellular jellies and tissues; a place where people merely "live." A few American cities, Manhattan chief among them, have some mad magnetic energy which sucks all others into "provincialism"; and Brooklyn of all great cities is nearest the magnet, and is indeed "provincial": it is provincial as a land of rich earth and of this earth is an enormous farm, whose crop is far less "industrial" or "financial" or "notable" or in any way "distinguished" or "definable" than it is of human flesh and being. And this fact alone, which of itself makes Brooklyn so featureless, so little known, to many so laughable, or so ripe for patronage, this fact, that two million human beings are alive and living there, invests the city in an extraordinarily high, piteous and inviolable dignity, well beyond touch of laughter, defense, or need of notice.

Manhattan is large, yet all its distances seem quick and available. Brooklyn is larger, seventy-one square miles as against twenty-two, but here you enter the paradoxes of the relative. You know, here: only a few miles from wherever I stand, Brooklyn ends; only a few miles away is Manhattan; Brooklyn is walled with world-traveled wetness on west and south and on north and east is the young beaverboard frontier of Queens; Brooklyn comes to an end: but actually, that is, in the conviction of the body, there seems almost no conceivable end to Brooklyn; it seems, on land as flat and huge as Kansas, horizon beyond horizon forever unfolded, an immeasurable proliferation of house on house and street by street; or seems as China does, infinite in time in patience and in population as in space.

The collaborated creature of the insanely fungoid growth of fifteen or twenty villages, now sewn and quilted edge to edge, and lacking any center in remote proportion to its mass, it is perhaps the most amorphous of all modern cities; and at the same time, by virtue of its arterial streets, it has continuities so astronomically vast as Paris alone or the suburbs south of Chicago could match: on Flatbush Avenue, DeKalb, Atlantic, New Lots, Church, any number more, a vista of low buildings and side streets of glanded living sufficient to paralyze all conjecture; simply, far as the eye can strain, no end of Brooklyn, and looking back, far as the eye can urge itself, no end, nor imaginable shore; only, thrust upon the pride of heaven, the monolith of the Empire State, a different mode of life; and even this, seen here, has the smoky frailty of a half-remembered dream.

(Observing in subway stations, in any part of Brooklyn, not in an hour of rush but in the leisured evening, you see this; how, wherever there is a choice of staircases, one toward Manhattan, one away, without thought or exception they descend the staircase toward the Island. An imaginative designer would have foreseen this and would have omitted the alternatives entirely.)

(In Upper Flatbush, already two miles deep inland from the bridges, a young woman of Manhattan asked a druggist how she might get into certain territory well south of there. Without thought of irony he began, "Oh. You want to go to Brooklyn.")

The center of population of the largest city in history is near the intersection of _____ and _____ Streets, in Brooklyn. That it should be in this borough of "being" rather than in that of doing and bragging seems appropriate to the point of inevitability. So does this: that when the fact was ascertained, and Manhattan news-swallows skimmed over to get the Local Angle, the replies were so fully intelligent that they had to be treated as a joke. Informed of his good fortune one said "So?", another said "So well?"; a landlady to be sure, said she'd have to tell her roomers about it that night, but gave evidence of no special emotion.

More homes are owned in Brooklyn than in any other Borough; there are more children per adult head; it is a great savings-bank town; there are fewer divorces; it is by and large as profoundly domesticated, docile and "stable" a population as one could conceive of, outside England. The horror of "unsuccessful" marriages—unsuccessful, that is, as shown by an open or legal break; the lethal effort of Carry On is thought well of—this horror is such that there is a special bank to which husbands come one day to deposit, estranged wives the next to be fertilized by this genteel equivalent of alimony.

It seems significant of Brooklyn that it is probably the only city that has such a bank.

At the north brow of Prospect Park, where a vast number of these marriages are, in the medical sense, contracted and where, indeed, the whole sweep of infancy, childhood, and the descending discords of family life is on display, there stands a piece of statuary. From a way down Flatbush Avenue it suggests that cloven flame which spoke with Dante in hell but by a nearer view, it is a man and a nude woman in bronze, and their plump child, eager for the Park, and it represents the beauty and stability of Brooklyn, and of human, family life. The man and wife stand back to back, in the classical posture of domestic sleep. It is a thoroughly vulgar and sincere piece of work, and once one gets beyond the esthete's sometimes myopic scorn, is the infallibly appropriate creation of the whole heart of Brooklyn. Michelangelo would have done much less well.

All the neighborhoods that make up this city; those well known, and those which are indicated on no official map:

The Hill, for instance: the once supremely solid

housing of Clinton Avenue, which are broken with a light titter of doctors' shingles; the two big homes which are become the L. I. Grotto Pouch and the Pouch Annex; or the boarded brownstone opposite the decrepitant bricks of the Adelphi Academy; or those blocks which have formed "protective associations" against the infiltration of Negroes:

Or Park Slope: the big Manhattan-style apartment buildings which now hem the Park, and on the streets of the upward slope, and on 8th Avenue, the bland powerful regiments of gray stone bays and the big single-homes, standing with a locked look among mature trees and the curious quietudes of bourgeois Paris: and these confused among apartment buildings and among parochial schools, and the yellow bricks of post-tenements, and the subway noises of "rough" children:

Or the Heights: the enormous homes and the fine rows, a steadily narrower area remains inviolable, the top drawer of Brooklyn, disintegration toward the stooping of the street the Squibb building: great houses broken apart for roomers; a gradual degeneration into artists and journalists, communists, bohemians and barbers, chiefly of Manhattan:

Or, among brownstones, between the last two-mile convergence of Fulton and Broadway, a swifter and swifter breakdown of the former middle classes, a steady thickening of Jews into the ultimacies of Brownsville and East New York:

Or that great range of brick and brownstone north of Fulton which in each two blocks falls more and more bad fortune: one last place, east of Fort Greene Park, the utmost magnificence of the brownstone style: and beyond-death at length in the Navy Yard district, the hardest in Brooklyn, harder even than Red Hook: (the hardest neighborhood in Brooklyn was a pinched labyrinth of brick and frame within a jump of Borough Hall, but the WPA cleared that one up:)

Or Eastern Parkway, the Central Park West of Brooklyn; in its first stretches near Prospect Park, the dwelling of the most potent Jews of the city; a slow then more swift ironing-out, and the end again in Brownsville:

Or Bay Ridge, and its genteel gentile apartment buildings, and the staid homes of Scandinavian seafarers:

Or Greenpoint and Williamsburg and Bushwick, the wood tenements, bare lots and broken vistas, the balanced weights and images of production and poverty; the headquarters of a municipal government as corrupt as any in the nation: everywhere the spindling Democratic clubs, the massive Roman churches; everywhere, in the eyes of men, in dark bars and on corners, knowledgeable appraising furtive light of hard machine politics; everywhere, the curious gas-lit odor of Irish-American democracy:

Or Flatbush: or Brighton: or Sheepshead Bay: or the negligible downtown: or the view, from the Fulton Street Elevated, of the low-swung and convolved sea of the living, as much green as roofs; or of Brooklyn's nineteenth century backyard life, thousands of solitaries, chips, each floated in his green eddy: or the comparable military attentions of the stoned dead, the stern hieroglyphs of Jews, the thousands of Gold Christs in the sun, the many churches focusing upon the frank secret star-demolished sky their steeplings and proud bulbs and triple crosses and sharp stars and squareflung roods moored high, light ballasted, among the harboring homes, ships pointing out the sun on a single wind: or the mother who walks on Division Avenue whose infant hexes her from his carriage in a gargoyle frown of most intense suspicion: or the street-writing on Park Slope: "Lois I have gone up the street. Don't forget to bring your skates.": or the soft whistling of the sea off Coney Island: or the façade of the Academy of Music, a faded print of Boston's Symphony Hall: or the young pair who face each other astride a bicycle in Canarsie: or the lavender glow of brownstones in cloudy weather, or chemical brilliance of jonquils in tamped dirt: or the haloed Sunday hats of little girls, as exquisite as those of their elders are pathologic: or the scornful cornices of dishonored homes: or the shade-cord at whose end is a white home-crocheted Jewish star: or the hot-pants little Manhattan sweat-shop girls who come to Tony's Square Bar to meet the sailors and spend a few bearable hours a week: or the streaming of first-flight gentiles from Poly Prep into Williams and Princeton, the second flight into Colgate or Cornell: or of the Jews whose whole families are breaking their hearts for it from Boys High into Brooklyn College and Brooklyn Law, and the luckies of them into Harvard: or the finance editor of the Eagle who believes all journalists are gentlemen who are out of what he calls the Chosen, and who scabbed in the Eagle strike: or in the middle afternoon in whatever part of Brooklyn, the star-like amplitude of baby buggies and of strolling and lounging silent or soft speaking women, the whole dwelling city as vacant of masculinity as most urgent war: or in his window above the banging of DeKalb Avenue late on a hot Saturday afternoon the grizzling skull-capped Jew who nods softly above the texts of his holiness, his lips moving in his unviolated beard, and who has been thus drowned in his pieties since early morning: or the grievings and the gracilities of the personalities at the zoo: or the bright fabric stretched of the confabulations of birds and children: or bed by bed and ward by ward along the sacred odors of the corridors of the twelve street mass of the Kings County Hospital, those who burst with unspeakable vitality or who are floated faint upon dubiety or who wait to die: These the sick, the fainted or fecund, the healthful, the young, the living and the dead, the buildings, the streets, the windows, the linings of the ward nests, the lethal chambers of the schools, the fumed and whining factories, the pitiless birds, the animals, that Bridge which stands up like God and makes music to himself by night and by day: all in the lordly, idiot light, These are inhabitants of Brooklyn:

Or Greenpoint: or Williamsburg: where from many mileages of the jungle of voided land, small factories, smokestacks, tenements, homes of irregular height and spacing, the foci are returned upon the eye, the blown dome and trebled crossage Greek church, and those massive gasoline reservoirs which seem to have more size than any building can: the hard trade avenues, intense with merchandisings of which none is above the taking of the working class: the bridal suites in modernistic veneers and hotcolored plushes, the dark little drugstores with smell like medicine spilled in a phone-booth mouth-piece: the ineffable baroques of gossamer in which little-girl-graduates and Brides of Heaven are clothed: Here and still strongly in Bushwick and persistent too in East New York and Brownsville, there is an enormous number of tall-windowed three- and four-floor wood houses of the fullblown nineteenth century, a style indigenous to Brooklyn, the façades as handsome as anything in the history of American architecture: of these, few have been painted within a decade or more, none are above the rooming house level, most are tenements, all are death-traps to fire: their face is of that half divine nobility which is absorptive of every humiliation, and is increased in each: many more of the tenements are those pallid or yellow bricks which are so much used all over Brooklyn as a mark of poverty: mixed among these many small houses of weathered wood, stucco, roofing: the stucco fronts are often Italian and usually uncolored, suggest nevertheless the rich Italianate washes; some are washed brick red, the joints drawn in white: or the golden oak doors of these neater homes, or the manifold and beautiful frontages of asphaltic shingles, some shinglings merely but applied in strong imaginations of color and pattern, others simulative of slate or brick and more handsome than either: the knowledge, forced on one, willing or no, that all street and domestic art is talented and powerful in proportion to poverty and disadvantage of blood: the care in the selection of curtains and windows ornaments: white shades and tasseled shade cords, or tan venetian blinds, or curtains of starched wrecked lace or red or gold or magenta sateen, little statues of comedy of faith, flowers, leaves and lamps: the names and faces of Irish, Italians, Jews and Slavs; and in the street the proud cries of children, the tightened eyes of fathers, the

dissolving beauties of young wives, the deep en-
thronements of the aged, and along five thousand
first floor windows in their gloom, ambushed behind drawn breathing shades, the staring into the
single zoned street of crouched aging women, the
look of tired lionesses in an endless zoo in a hot
afternoon: and in the bleeding of early neons, the
return of the typists; and of the students in careful
suits, hard ties, carrying their toxic books, and the
small bare crowding, where men gentle with
weariness drink beer in the solace of each other's
voices and the nickelodeon: and in the evenings,
here almost in the warm Hebraic volubilities of
Brownsville, such a swarm, affection, patience,
bitterness and vitality in existence as words will
not record:

Or the drive one afternoon, with a Brooklyn
journalist, a too-well-born young man not long
enough out of Harvard: which began in the vi-
brated shelters of Brooklyn Bridge and threaded
the waterfront and at length sketched in motion
the whole people of Brooklyn: the shore drive along
Bay Ridge, Coney Island, Sheepshead Bay, and in
darkness drove the narrow vision of its needle
steep northward through the whole body of the

city, straight through Flatbush: those who gathered firewood on a vacant lot on Front Street: the huge warehouses, their walls a yard thick, which were built in the time of the clipper ships: a harvester addressed to Guaraquito, a Chevrolet on its way to Peru, stacks of scrap iron ready for loading to kill whom, where, this time: the calm leaning above earth of the *Hulda Maerak, Isbrandtsen Moller*, the effulgence of her pale aluminum, her beautifully made bow: pine refugee crates, all of the utmost size permitted for the bringing way of the inappraisable objects of outrage, grief and remembrance, veiled in tarpauline as if they were deaths and marked with that wineglass which is this planet's symbol for this end up: it is memorable, too, how half the houses in this section are deserted, the windows shattered, standing jagged as war among vacant lots, the ghosts of floors against their walls: and the dark hard bars at street corners, and men who watched the bland progress of this skimming-sedan in cold strychnine deeply gratifying hate: and along the sheltered Atlantic Basin the warehouses stored with newsprint from Nova Scotia, Norway, Latvia, Finland: and further down the front the ships from South America and

Africa and Japan: in the middle of a vacant lot a Negro who sat on a lard can and ate out of a newspaper: the mahogany odors of roasting coffee: the prow of the *Tai Yin*, *Ionsberg*, dark as a planned murder above a heap of scrap: the funereally rusted prows also of the *Dundrum Castle* and the *Ohio*: how little of Grover Whalen there is in the clothing of the customs officials of a freight waterfront: how relaxed work is here as against the Manhattan waterfront, almost the sun-saturated ease of New Orleans: an enormous repaired Diesel gentled along on a Williamsburg hauler, suggesting, in the middle of the street, an extracted heart: the negroid breath of a molasses factory: a glimpse of the Red Hook housing project which may or may not, unlike all former American housing projects, serve those for whom it is intended: on the curve of a new cinder track nine strong boys aslant in distance running, their aura part ancient Greece part present Leningrad: the pale parade of the great structures of the Bush Terminal, powerful as barges: the hulls resting where the olive shipments used to be heavy: the journalist's efforts to get to the yachting docks ("the *Corsair* sometimes docks here"), but "they keep them pretty well barricaded":

the long jetty created of the ballast of returning clippers, stacked now with Pacific Coast lumber: the cheap white-sweated brick of the Red Hook Play center: or the skinned land which was formerly a Hooverville, available to the totally derelict, but which under squarer dispensation wears WPA's usual creditline for having Cleaned this Area: or how the comfortable young man remarked of certain outrageously poor homes left standing, that they were not of the squatter class; these people have some right to be here but (laughing) imagine you or I living in such a way: and the drawbridge over the Gowanus Canal, its sheathings and angularities in motion as elegant as those of a starved cat: or how he remarked that one may find a good deal of prose in Brooklyn but precious little poetry, or again, of the whole region just traversed, "Good solid work here; no swank; not a part of town one comes to see much, but quite necessary to the community":

Or further, along the shore road, passing a stretch of rather Ducky middle-income houses, the "Tudor" type, his patronizing approval; "Here at least you can see some *attempt* at decency"; and a half-made park with the odd pubescent nudity of all new public efforts; and on the Bay the pinched island Fort Lafayette with the minelaying equipment, and Hoffman's Island, the quarantine for parrots and monkeys: the obsolete cannons of Fort Hamilton: a shut-down deserted block of middle-class housing of the twenties: the blasted mansions of Victorian pleasaunce, boarded or brokenout with gasolines and soft drinks: the San Carlo Bocce-Drome, rubbed earth in oilgreen tree shade, soft stepping middleaged Italians at play: a dismantled country club: the high mild-breezed lift of the shore drive:

And on Coney, the drive along a back street past dirtied frames which suggest the poorer parts of the Jersey Shore and which are said to be the worst "slum" in Greater New York; and his speaking, with limitless scorn and hatred, of Sea Gate, a *restricted* neighborhood; the *aristocracy, Mrs. Linkowitz, Mrs. Finkelstein*; and Sea Gate itself, at the west end of the island, a few wooden victorians, the rest undersized pretensions of gaudiest most betraying bricks, perhaps the most dreadfully piteous excrescence crystallization of snobbery I have ever seen; and in a barren place at the far end of the island, in a bright spring sun of six o'clock, the engine quiet, and the whole of the Harbor paved the color of dawn and deep up the north the slow laboring pencil-mark shadow of an outgoing liner, and at profound distance, spoken out of the ocean water itself, a whistling, and light tolling:

And how at Landy's in Sheepshead Bay he outlined his plans for solidifying himself in the community before joining the Nazi *Bund*:

And in darkness, the deep, droned drive up the whole façade of the scarcely distinguishable city; the ascent of a diving bell:

And the hesitations and slow drivings around Brooklyn College: along the walk next the ball field entrance the slowly moving crowd and the lighted placards with the key words, UNITY? WAR; and the new-appearing buildings of this great day college, bloomed with light of study, bad Georgian, the look of a unit of Harvard houseplans with elephantiasis; and again skirting the ball field, trying to hear; in the middle of the field was one dark group and a speaker raised among them with his Flag, on the far side another such group (could they be opponents?) , and the placards; and again along the side of the field, as near as we could get, the fat motor idling, and the driver speaking hatefully of

22

Jews; five students came along the walks glancing over, and crossed away in front of us, one of them saying "the Communist sons of bitches"; there was a thin mist through which all light seemed meager and the sky enormous, and in the faint field they stood dark, earnestly attentive, their placards oscillating; and above them, with the help I believe of a weak microphone, came the passionate incompetent speaking of the student. From where we were only his deep sincerity and fear and the inadequacies of his particular mind and intonations were at first audible, but at length the grayed desperate salient words came through, in his brave uncertain hypnotized tenor, "war" . . . "democracy" . . . "unalterably opposed"; and the placards moved as masts in a harbor: it was the night before Hitler was to tell Roosevelt there would be no ten years' peace, and I suggested that that must be the cause of the mass meeting. The journalist agreed it must be, added "Let them, Let them yap about peace and democracy all they like. They're not going to impress Hitler one little bit."

(All over the city on streets and walks and walls the children, and the other true primitives of the race have established ancient, essential and ephemeral forms of art, have set forth in chalk and crayon the names and images of their pride, love, preying, scorn, desire; the Negroes, Jews, Italians, Poles, most powerfully, these same poorest most abundantly, and in these are the characters of neighborhood and of race: on an iron door in Williamsburg: *Dominick says he will Fuck Fanny*. On another: *Boys gang up on Don* and *Down with Don* and *Don is a Bull Artist*. Against green shingles of a Bushwick side door: *The Lady in this House is Nuts*. In an immaculate neighborhood of lower middle class Jews in East New York, against a new blood wash of drugstore brick, the one word *strike*. On a Bensonhurst street, bourgeois Jewish: *Bernice Davidson is the future Mrs. Allan Cunn. She may be the future Mrs. Henry Eiseman*. In Brighton, among Jews recently withdrawn from the ghetto, a child begins an abstract drawing and his mother quickly: "*Don't* do-that," and a ten-year-old boy immediately, to a younger, in the same notation, "*Don't* do-that." On Park Slope on a Sunday afternoon, not printed, but in an unskillful Palmer script: *Lois I have gone up the street. Don't forget to bring your skates.* In Williamsburg: *Ruby loves Max but Max* HATES *Ruby*.

And drawings, all over, of phalli, fellatio, ships, homes, airplanes, western heroes, women, and monsters dredged out of the memories of the unspeakable sea-journeys of the womb, all spangling the walks and walls, which each strong shower effaces.)

Or deep in Flatbush; in a warm *middle* afternoon.

I leave the trolley avenue and walk up a residential street: I have not gone a block before I recognize a silence so powerful and so specialized it has almost a fragrance of its own: it is the silence of having left a street of the open world and of having entered an empty church, and is much that fragrance: and there is in the silence an almost Brahmin tranquility, weakening to the senses, and a subtly terrifying quality of suffocation and of the sacrosanct: and in a moment more, standing between these rows of neat homes, I know what this special sanctitude is: that this world is totally dedicated to tame marriages in their first ten years of youth, and that during the sweep of each working day these streets are yielded over to housewives and to young children and to infants so entirely, that those who stroll these walks and sit in the sun are cloistral nuns, vestals, made fecund though they are, and govern a world in which returning men are made womanly in an odor of cherished floors, clean cloths, nationally advertised cosmetics, and the sharp stench of babies. Two youths, it is true, toss a ball back and forth in the street; but they do so as if this were a puritan sunday, or an area of crisis in sickness in which for relief the healthful must relax, but gently; the rest is as I have said: I see five closed cars, moored empty before doors: each is lately washed, the treads of the tires are sharp, they are all black, not one but is a Chevrolet, Ford or Plymouth: and on doorsteps dolls and the bright aerodynamic toys of the children of this decade: and it seems before every house, shining hearselike in the glare, an identical perambulator, deep, black, sleek with lacquer, brimmed with white cloths: and women: two who stroll abreast along the shadowless adolescence of saplings, serving their carriages; two more who sit in an open door and talk in stopped-down voices; another who sits alone, addling the sprung carriage and staring emptily upon the street; another who, drawing aside a sunporch curtain, peers out upon my watching with the soft sterile alarm of one whose knight is east crusading: a laundry truck sneaks cushioning past and halts at a far door; far up the street I hear the voice of a child; in his shaded pram by the step, swollen with royalty, a baby sleeps; a half mile up Flatbush Avenue, the metal whine of a northbound trolley:

Some of the houses are ten to fifteen years old, some are much younger; all, in their several ways, perfect images of these matings: little doubles and singles of brick and shingle or of brick and stucco or of solid brick in rows: of these latter, five in a row, rather new, are cautiously ornate and are fronted in nearpatterns of bright brick the six colors of children's modeling clays: they are so prim, so undersized, they suggest dolls' homes or the illustrations of a storybook of pretty dreams for sexually ripened children; or as if through some kind white magic they had been made of candy, to the wonder and delight of two who, lost and loving in a wilderness, came suddenly upon a home: "exposed" "beams," wrought-iron knockers, white concrete steps, oak doors with barred peeping-shutters, little touches of the Elizabethan, the Colonial, the Byzantine: or the others, those peaked twins faced with shingles, or those of which the porch is wood glass and brick, the first floor stucco, above that weatherboard or shingle: and of these kinds each has a sunporch, and at the door two whitewashed urns or boxes for flowers, and each a little six-by-four lawn and a low hedge: and these lawns are brightly seeded, and shrubbed with dark junipers, and are affectionately tended: and in the curtained or venetianblinded windows of these sunporches there are bullfrogs and pelicans and scotch terriers and swans of china and roadside potteries of green or yellow sprouting streaked reptilian leaves at whose roots are dainty cowries: and between the homes, or between each double, a streakless concrete lane, exactly wide enough between the windowless walls to pass the sedan, and beyond, a garage; and in these backyards, bright in the sun on patented lines, the bedspreads and the pastelled undergarments of women to whom the natural-color advertisements have told their love of nice things, and this washing has been done in supreme suds which are incapable of damaging the most delicate fabrics and which keep these women unenvious of one another's hands, in electric machines which would flatter any motion picture's conception of a laboratory in an essay on the holiness of medical students:

Or more ordinarily perhaps, few or none of the most fairystory of these lovenests, but solid regiments of the other types, or mixtures of types; both the uniform and the varied strongly exist: plain cubed double-houses of dark red or brindled brick of the twenties is one kind, very common; another, the wood doubles whose twin peaked gables make an M above the partitioned sunporch; and some are faced entirely with stucco; and more often than not there is scarcely room between the walls for a child to get through and the sidewalk trees are developed well beyond the sapling stage; and quite frequently, too, there is at the corner a four- or a six-floor brick apartment building, with a small cement court in which the women sit in camp or windsor chairs; and from one or two windows of these, some pouting betrayal of humility, a cerise mattress; or again for no good reason these buildings will thicken to occupy most of several blocks and there will be fewer mattresses and women at the sills or none and a higher rental, and fewer hatless women in spring coats over housedresses; on some streets there is an inexplicable mixture of "classes," and of "grades" of homes, Central Europeans, a sudden family of Negroes in

a scarred frame house, facing the most laxatived of
Anglo-Saxons; or again scarce-explicably, a block
of solid working class, a row of upper porches,
where a rubbertree takes the air and a child's
stained sheets are spread, and a woman combs and
fondles in the sun her long wild ivory ghastly hair
whose face, peering from this ambush, is the four
staring holes of a drowned corpse, and the boys
play ball more loudly and of two little boys, passing on limber legs, one is saying, just above a whis-
per, "... you know: back stairs. You know: down the
back stairs. Back stairs. You know: ..." and at the
end of the street a small factory without even a
name moans like many flies: Or, too, there are
streets of spaced homes, side lawns and heavy trees
whose structures are columned wood, wide plates
of glass, big porches, the thick sundaydinner pro-
prieties which succeeded the jigsaw period: or
rows again of yellow brick, flatfaced or roundly
bayed, rented dwellings, such as may be seen in
every part of Brooklyn and in much of the eastern
United States:—enough variety, mixture, monot-
ony, sudden change, that it is impossible to gener-
alize Flatbush: and in all this variety nevertheless
and in the actions and faces of those who live here

the drive of an all but annihilative, essential uniformity: such that it seems, that the middle class suburbs and residential streets of all the small cities of the continent are here set against one another and ironed to one scarcely wrinkled flatness and similitude. The "avenues," the arteries, are no less like themselves: immeasurable stretches of three floor yellow brick with ground floor merchants of hosiery and exlax—for Brooklyn's "downtown," too, is ironed thin to every door: and in this lowness of all building and in the almost stellar vistas of the avenues, an incredible dilation of the sky and the flat horizon, and thus, paradoxic with the odors of suffocation, the open grandeurs almost of a ranch, the quietudes not only of paralysis but of the stratosphere: and so it is not surprising in a Flatbush husband that he feels the air is a lot cleaner out here; a decent place to raise your kids.

(In the gallery of one of the big second-run theaters in the downtown section of Flatbush Avenue, about ten in the evening, they were nearly all high school boys. They all knew each other, as they don't in New York, and kept calling across to each other, and the way they tried to pick up my wife (she was alone) was different from New York, too: "Hey miss what time is it" and "Hey miss what's your first name." They teased the picture more volubly, too. It was a very ordinary thoroughbred show, Kentucky etcetera, with the customary crimes against the talents of Zasu Pitts; but there was one sequence, a spring night, when the heroine was called from a party and waited, glowing in the darkness in her evening dress, while a champion colt was foaled, of a dying dam. Small-lighted men labored intensely in the dark stable over a dark mass almost in silence, and in the gabby balcony an extraordinary quiet, tender, premonitory incertitude took full hold. Out of this gentle, intuitive, questioning silence at length, in a mild naked voice, a boy in the front row realized: "The horse is having a baby." And a boy five rows back, in a thickened voice, cried: "Aww, why don't you shut *up*.")

Social note.

Brooklyn Heights: the dusk of the Gods.

It was really very kind of them, but one can't help that; or must one. The façade was Heights 19th Century, but the extent of the daughter's revolt consisted in a renegade taste for the smuggest and safest in modernism, so the interiors were a little beyond her parents. They both had tall large narrow faces, and an almost oriental cruelty in the eyes and the ends of the lower lips: like many married couples each suggested an unflattering reflection of the other, and they had the strange corpsy dryness common to all whose living is contractive, antihuman. There were weak sidecars served by the usual gentle, refined, ruined girl of foreign extraction, one drink each and a half glass over for me, and we went down to dinner. On a wide dry plate lay four high-grade Cattleyas, all directed at me; but I made no comment. The bay was softlighted against fair slender palms, and the curtains, with that ostentatious good taste which is the worst taste of all, were drawn against the most magnificent view in greater New York. We ate exquisitely cooked boned squab, pecansized potatoes fried in a fine oil, asparagus without sauce, and an exceptionally good dessert of strawberries, baked eggwhite and icecream whose aggregate name I lack the worldly wisdom to know: Baked Alaska, probably: and as the food came and went I developed the feeling, perhaps unfairly, that this was not the ordinary Tuesday evening menu, and that the specialization was the result less of hospitality than of the wish to astound the bourgeois. Unfortunately the thing I think of most is the rotted meat which is freshened with embalming fluid and sold at a feasible price to the Negroes along Fulton Street who, lacking the benefits of a thorough course in biology, and any other sniff at it while they are yet conscious, are not in a position to identify this odor as the alter ego of death. While we ate she talked. There is no room here to tell of it all. (I refer you to Swift's *Polite Conversation*), but of some little it is impossible to refrain. About the private park, for instance, which the survivor of the Misses Pierrepont still holds open to the play of the appropriate children, each of whose mothers is given a key, on the strict condition, of course, that no little friends be brought in, or not without express permission. Gramercy Park; yes; but so much more dear and, private. Of course you've heard of the Stuart Washington; the one Lafayette spoke of as the best likeness. (So dear and private.) And at Bellport, my youngest has struck up the sweetest relationship with (a hardware merchant): calls him (by an upper-class seaboard style pet name). I asked, with malice aforethought in the ambiguity, whether it is "mixed" at Bellport. She stiffened a little but recovering: "Oh no: they're all Americans."

(One up for me, fat lady.) Of course heaven knows nowadays *what* one's daughters meet at Packer. Yet of course (yes of course) they learn to form their own groups; it's really rather a good exposure, rather a good training; after all, they'll have to be doing just that all their lives. (I nod. I think of the poor rich daughters of jewelers and contractors whose parents are responsible: and what is responsible for that crime in the parents.) And of course the Institute. (I pretend never to have heard of it.) 'Why the institute of Arts and *Sciences*: . . . splendid . . . wonderful . . . Academy of Music . . . Boston Symphony lectures . . . the Academy is filled whenever William Lyon Phleps (discovers Browning) . . . But of late, I gather, this is cracking. The new director insists on everyone's *mixing*; it's for *all* Brooklyn; of course there must be really *lovely* people on the *Hill*, and *Park Slope*, and down in *Flatbush*, *whom* one might never hear of otherwise, but really . . . one meets one's hairdresser . . . in brief, it appears that those ladies whose pleasurable illusion has been that the bloody distillations of the fury, innocence and the genius of the planet are their particular property are beginning to lose interest in "culture," that masked antichrist which in fact is of itself more than they have ever possessed.

After dinner there is no coffee: tardily, and with slight begrudging, cordials are offered, a choice of green chartreuse and Grand Marnier. I am shown a charming glass-painting of early New York superior to any in the City Museum, decline a cigar (courteously) and am led upstairs to the library, and the serious talk of the evening. At the stairhead she turns, her voice lowered and sparkling in a hint of roguishness, by indescribable subtleties of manner Leads me, as such women Lead: "Mr ____ ; oh Mr. A. I do hope when you write of Brooklyn you (beckoning) *won't* say that *all* the bedrooms in Brooklyn are (beckoning) dreadful, sordid, stuffy little places; (her voice still more lowered: opening a door:) look here":

The room is perhaps twenty-five by fifteen; the broad panes command the harbor and the complete lower island; the bed is low to the floor and eight feet square. I wonder what possible use it can be to them, and think of the limitations which poverty sets round the clean sensual talents of Jews and Negroes.

As we leave she reiterates, with just a touch of

blackmail in the voice, her eager anticipation of the article, which she will most certainty read. I hope, madam, that it was not mere courtesy: and I wish I might have served more of your friends, however unimportant they may be.

I think I remember more vividly, though, her re-mark: ". . . *dreadful* neighborhood; dreadful: Ne-groes on Myrtle Avenue: Syrians within two blocks of us, nudging our elbows: I *do wish they'd clear them away.*"

The first settlers of what was to become Brooklyn landed on the Heights in 1636. By 1642 the only In-dians on Long Island were huddled on the damp prow of Montauk Point.

Thirty-four years ago, when Mr. George Hobson, a gentle resident of the Hill neighborhood, began teaching Latin in Boys High School, there was hardly a Jew to be seen in the corridors.

Today one sixteenth of the world's whole of the Jewish people reside in Brooklyn and comprise half the population of that city. If "society" in the Heights—Society meaning-of-the-word—has any significance whatever, which is at least open to ques-tion, every simple realist must agree that the Jewish "society" of the Eastern Parkway and the St. George ball and banquet room is incomparably more important, more powerful and more dignified than that which crouches at the crumbling edge of the Heights.

It is a pleasure to know that neither is quite acceptable among equivalent New Yorkers: and that the latter are still less securely presentable before both God and Man.

(Or, opposite a loud concrete playground in East New York, sitting in the kind sun in his infinitesimal lawn in a kitchen rocker, his dirty brocaded bathrobe drawn tight, the wasted workman of forty whose face still wears the alien touch of death: his chin is drawn in as far as it will go and he is staring with eyes like diamonds upon the vitalities of the schoolboys, frowning with furious sorrow, his mouth caught up one cheek in a kicking smile:)

Or in Bay Ridge, a sweet quiet of distance from the city, a flag staff in the water breeze, the many apartment buildings ornate but in the self-playing nordic taste; the young woman waiting in the maroon roadster; the mother and child who stand at the subway mouth; and each five minutes, in a walking noise of dry leaves, the rising from underground of the gently or complacently docile: the young woman loses patience and drives away; the mother and her husband do not kiss when they meet; two middle aged men come up talking together, but most of those who rise thus from the dead give no appearance of knowing one another but walk alone toward their suppers; and the unimaginable solitude of most families begins to suggest itself:

Or Bensonhurst, those double and single homes and whole towns of apartments of not unprosperous Jews along the well-shaded streets, as affable among one another, almost, as in the ghettos; the well-pleased wives, the sexuality in the eyes and garments of the high school girls, the exceedingly richly fed children, their thighs thick in their trousers, the father who sits in his small lawn, his eyes naphthaline with ruinous adoration of his boy; the plump blond boys who pitch ball quietly in the street, with excellently cushioned gloves of yellow leather; the college student, trying to cancel his dark opulent features in sharp tweeds; the five mothers, and seven children in an apartment court who all eat ice cream cones, all raspberry; the adolescent girl on the front steps whose eyes, glanced upward, are at once hot and pure; the reappearance of the tweed student, licking an ice cream cone, raspberry flavor:

Or Brighton Beach, the flatfaced apartments chilled in their own shade and the gay candy-colored brick homes, in every one a room for rent, and the almost shacklike bungalows, and the parents watching for their children in front of the school; the hot orange and blue trim of the houses, the diminutive synagogues:

Or Sheepshead Bay, the blunt little launches still trestled, the colors and shapes of children's paintings; the hopeless desolation of the worn-out edge of Brooklyn; the criminally-made row houses in the middle of nowhere; the desperately pathetic matchwood shacks stilted above the stench of the mudflats; the manhole turrets rising to that level at which Robert Moses will establish another of his parks, with reflecting pools, and an end of the shacks:

Or Canarsie, that full end-of-the-world, that joke even to Brooklyn, its far end; the abomination of desolation, the houses thinned to nothing, the blank sand, the shattered cabaret with the sign, "The Girl You Bring is the Girl You Take Home," the new cabaret in the middle of waste silence, with ambitious men aligning the brilliant trims; the shades along the last street and at its head a small young brick apartment, its first floor occupied; the row of dark peaked shingles which across a little park faces the declining sun and the bare land with the look: "somehow we have not been very success-ful in life"; and this park itself, brand-new, a made-island of green in all this grave ocean, and in this silence, a little noise: The leaves are blown aslant and in their shade a few lie prostrate on young grass, mothers, young girls, two boys together; and meditate, or talk inaudibly; on benches, men with-out color sit apart from one another in silence. A girl bounces a fat ball on the cement over and over and over. The wind is freshening and the sloped light is turning gold. Birds speak with each other in the hushed leaves and in the wind there are the soft calls of children, but these noises are blown by the wind and are finally almost impossible to hear.

In Prospect Park on Sunday they are all there, on the lake, along the bending walks, sown on the seas of lawn; the old, the weary, the loving, and the young; who move in the flotations of seeds upon placid winds: a family, gathering its blankets and its baskets, quarreling a little: Four young men hatless in dark coats walk rapidly across the vast grass in an air of purpose and of enigma: a little boy running alone who suddenly leaps into the air: another little boy and an elderly man and a rolled umbrella, hand in hand: the rear end of a metal swan, a tractor saddle and bicycle pedals: a working class father of fifty who, leant to a tree, holds four identical hats by their elastics and watches toward the water with an iron and tender look: two little girls stand on two stones by the ruffed water and hesitate toward one another like courting insects: an old woman built like a bear sits alone on a bench with her fecund spread and her hands folded on her belly; she is intensely watching everything in sight and in silence the tears run freely down her face: three boys and three hardfleshed girls in working-class clothes range past with the resourceful and sensitive eyes of wild animals: four couples in file, unaware of one another, push baby carriages along a walk; three are sombre, one is mutual: a young man suddenly genuflects before a smiling girl in a gold blouse, his hands at the eye at his heart like a tenor: six delicately dressed Negro boys of eight to fourteen softly follow a seventh who pushes a virgin bicycle of cream and ultramarine and gold with an unsullied squirrel's tail smoking at the heel of the rear mud-guard: he does not ride but continually hovers his lovely machine with the passion of a stallion and the reverence of a bridegroom; his eyes are dazed, and he is unspeakably touched and solitary: the young man, his photograph made, gets up and dusts his knee: within this range of lawn, each at wide distance from the others, five children are running rapidly with the young child's weakness at the knee; not one, from here, is larger than a gnat: in a deep walk alone, a boy with a meek nape abruptly kisses his thicklegged girl and they laugh and kiss again; she digs her dark head deeply against his neck and with arms tightened they walk on with the unsteadiness of drunks: in a walk alone, in the beauty of the Botanic Gardens, an elderly woman stands very still facing a robin who stands still, dabs at the pavement, and points his eye at her; when she is seen the woman smiles slyly yet timorously, as a child might who feared reprimand: all over those long drawn heaving of fair lawn each mirroring the whole mystery of one another's past and being and future and each blind to the signals of warning they move in hundreds and in thousands in such spaciousness they scarcely seem a crowd but a whole race dispread upon a fresh green world, and their motions upon this space are those of a culture upon a microscopic slide:

(And one by one, slowly disclosed in the speed of walking of Washington Avenue and the slow withdrawal of an apartment cornice, in gradual parade upon the facade of the Institute of Arts and Science and upon the iron sky, letter by letter, figure by figure, the names and images of the noble: Confucious: Lao-tze: Moses: David: Jeremiah: Isaiah: St. Peter: St. Paul: Mohammed: and, between columns, each: Sophocles: Pericles: Herodotus: Thucydides: Socrates: Demosthenes:

The great gray building static, the sky is slowly crowded to the left:

Or late in the day, in the zoo, the black bears with the muzzles of vaudeville tramps, and those who affectionately watch them: the empty pit: the desperate bawlings of the single polar bear, his eyes half crazy with loneliness, his whole focus on the pit of blacks: the quieting and softening of all light and the wonder this performs upon some animals: the sexy teasings and huggings of the round masked brighteyed coons and the delight there must be in the wrestlings of fat furred bodies: the deep moat where Hilda the elephant was pushed by her playful husband, to die in bewilderment of sacroiliac pain, and where he too recently fell: that cage in which three black metal eagles, hunchbacked with heart-cracking melancholia, fall clumsy as grounded buzzards from limb to limb of their small skinned tree, "Presented to the Children of New York by the Brooklyn Daily Eagle": and through the dusk the agonies of the bear; *Baw*: *Baww*: *Bawwww*!: and the bumpings and kiddings of the gay coons: and the kangaroos, some orange, and some fawn, whose eyes are lovely as those of giraffes or of victorian heroines and who move like wheelchairs: and the deer:

It is late dusk now, with the lamps on; the sky is one clean pearl. There are almost no people left. Those kingly anarchists who have become symbols of journalism sit quite without motion. The bear is still crying: he has the sound of a baby who has been forgotten in the attic of an abandoned house. In their run the young among the deer are altered. They are no longer being watched and it is not only that: they are caught also at the heart and throughout their bodies with that breath-depriving mystical ecstasy which dusk excites in them and in young goats. Their eyes are sainted, innocent, as those of goats daemonic. They move tenderly, with a look of minnows about the head and body: then a sudden break, a strong-sprung sharphooved bouncing run in the soft dirt, the precisions of chisels and of Mozart: and in the midst of this one of them will suddenly leap high into the air, wrists high, tail waggling, wriggling his whole body upon itself in a blind spasm of self-delight (while the kangaroos amble and squat) : and now, even; it is rapidly darkening: in a child's angry joy in life and furious reluctance in the death even of one day, a fawn tears out again on the empty run and three times over climbs the air and congratulates himself: and out of the fallen brightness of the air, low a long while then steadily rising, hammered and beaten mad hell with ceremonial bells, drawn in a whole periphery of this green park and this world, such a wild inexhaustible wailing as to freeze the root of the heart.

1939

JAMES RUFUS AGEE was born in a working-class section of Knoxville, Tennessee, on November 27, 1909, the son of Hugh James Agee and Laura Whitman Tyler. His father's death in an automobile accident when Agee was seven deeply affected him throughout his life.

In 1918, Laura Agee moved the family to St. Andrews, Tennessee, enrolling her son in an Episcopalian monastic school. There Agee met an important spiritual and intellectual influence, Father James Harold Flye. Now a classic, their extensive correspondence was published in 1961 as *Letters of James Agee to Father Flye,* and the collection paints a superb portrait of Agee.

In 1925, Agee entered Phillips Exeter Academy. He graduated and went on to Harvard College, where he wrote stories and poems, and, for the *Harvard Advocate,* a parody of *Time* magazine that won him a position as a reporter at *Fortune* magazine, where he worked from 1932 to 1937. In 1936, *Fortune* assigned Agee and the photographer Walker Evans to do a piece on southern sharecroppers. They spent two months in rural Alabama and gave the magazine a document it decided not to publish. Agee left *Fortune* and reworked the article into *Let Us Now Praise Famous Men,* first published in 1941. The book was well received critically, but sold poorly. In subsequent editions, the book became established as a documentary masterpiece.

In 1939 and by now a fixture of the New York left-literary community, Agee was assigned by *Fortune* to write an article on Brooklyn for a special issue on New York. Agee moved to Flatbush, renting an apartment on St. James Place for two months in the winter and spring of 1939. *Fortune* did not publish Agee's piece, entitled "Southeast of the Island:

Travel Notes," deeming it "too strong to print," in the words of his friend, the critic Robert Fitzgerald. The magazine replaced Agee's article with one by another writer, and the piece remained unpublished until it ran under the title "Brooklyn Is" in *Esquire* in 1968.

Nearly broke, Agee joined Fitzgerald at *Time* as a book reviewer in 1939. Two years later, he became a movie reviewer—first at *Time*, and then at *The Nation* from 1942 to 1948, where he shaped a new style of film criticism that combined authority with a demotic enthusiasm for the art. By the late 1940s, Agee had become an accomplished screenwriter, collaborating with John Huston on *The African Queen* and with Charles Laughton on *The Night of the Hunter.* During these years, however, his already difficult personal life—and addictions to smoking, drinking, and stimulants—began to take a toll, as Agee suffered a round of heart attacks. Agee died of a heart attack while in a taxicab in New York City on May 16, 1955—the same day his father had died thirty-nine years earlier.

In 1957, Agee was awarded the Pulitzer Prize for *A Death in the Family,* the novel about his childhood, and the impact of his father's death, that he struggled unsuccessfully to complete for more than twenty years. Its immensely powerful, lyrical evocation of loss in a boy's Knoxville of 1915–1916 is Agee's greatest work, and an American classic.